M000083293

Beauty Noticed

Poems by

Catherine R. Seeley

ISBN 978-1-62806-295-3 (print | paperback)

Library of Congress Control Number 2020917956

Published by Salt Water Media
29 Broad Street, Suite 104
Berlin, MD 21811
www.saltwatermedia.com

Cover design by Salt Water Media. Cover image by unsplash.com user Jovica Ilievski. Interior images by unsplash.com users Kai Pilger, Daniel Straub, and Jens Johnsson

Beauty Noticed

Acknowledgements

My thanks to the Eastern Shore Writers Association for the selection and inclusion of my poem, "Eire," in the anthology, *Bay to Ocean 2019: The Year's Best Writing from the Eastern Shore* and for inclusion of my poem, "The Waterman's Son," in the 2020 anthology, *Bay to Ocean: The Year's Best Writing from the Eastern Shore*.

For

Alexa, Anna, Aoife, Ashley, Bonnie Kathleen, Brynn, Carmelia, Caroline, Casey, Coco, Doireann, Ella, Emily, Emma, Fiona, Gabby, Genna, Grace, Harriet, Isabelle, Jessica, Julia, Kate, Katy, Lila, Neasa, Orla, Rachel, Rebecca, Reese, Roisin, Seren, Shea, Skye, and Violetta:

Young girls today; bright leaders tomorrow.

Contents

Eire

High upon the Cliffs of Moher,
At Dingle and at Slea Head,
Up in Sligo, Benbulben's glen,
In Clonmacnois along the Shannon,
My disposition turns mendicant
Begging earth, wind, sun and sea
To so fill the coffer of my senses
With the memories of their drama
That such visions may never be spent
And I shall be spared the parting.

Farmers Must Know

What do farmers know that we passersby do not?
Perhaps they only know parents' wishes for them
That, one day, they'd inherit the land and prosper.
Gift or sentence, they soon will discover which.

How must it be to stand before such a mass of land,
Wondering what to sow, what to risk, where to begin,
Why one should gamble so much for another's good,
When droughts, floods or frost can threaten ruin?

When late summer sun catches the buttery glistening
Of sweet kernels of corn slipping down grateful chins
Does a wave of beneficence buoy their tired limbs,
Swell their hearts, since fruit of their toil spoils us?

While they stop and look out over an acre of woods
Do their eyes see the trees inhale six tons of CO_2,
Exhale four tons of oxygen so just eighteen humans
Breathe a year's clean air, thanks to their stewardship?

Who better can intuit subterranean covenants made
Between soil and shoots than the weathered agrarian,
Whose vigilance and genius turn fields into banquets
Minds to heaven, hearts to the needy, families to table.

The Story of Creation

In the beginning,
God created.
Hanging lanterns in caverns
Snapping shades on windows,
Flooding light into dark and shadow.
"Rise and shine!" The call
Barreling down the tunnel of time
Drifting into the ear of one
Who would flinch with sudden start
At what was thought to have been heard.

In the beginning,
God created.
Measuring off farmlands and building sites:
Mustard seeds and temples were in mind.
With the scrutiny of a surveyor,
Those measuring eyes saw
What ours still might not:
The imperceptible seedlings of goodness
Poked into the ground of everything.

In the beginning,
God created.
Sculpting from the void a form,
From the mass an image
Revealing, as artists do
In the naming of each work,
The signing of every piece,
A covetousness for what hand had hewn.

In the beginning,
As if having a premonition
Regarding future dissent,
The lamplighter, shade lifter,
Ground breaker, clod sculptor,
God rested while she could.

Sacred Universe

Sacred universe,
How does my world eclipse you?
Forgive me, old friend

Original Sin

"This indeed is very good!"
Satisfactorily sighed the Creator.
Limitations and talents,
Liabilities and skills:
Great gizzards of human nature!

"Yes, this indeed is very good!"
Admiringly gazed the Maker.
Rain forests, Himalayas,
Serengeti and seas:
Earth's perfectly balanced nature.

"Not good enough!" Or, "I disagree!"
The original sin that lingers.
And so gets trashed
The landscape within
As well as the world to cinders.

Beauty Noticed

Wounds abound, but beauty noticed heals.
The curl inside the wave, its foamy luminance
Over-arching all aches, lifts and carries
Even the resistant to some shore of relief.

Or, if land locked in some desert of dilemma,
Giant cumulus above the barren stretch
Turn heads upward, cajoling and diverting
Downcast eyes to look up, beyond for a time.

Crises paralyze, but beauty noticed heals.
The baton poised to summon Tchaikovsky,
Whose tapestry of notes drapes 'round weary souls,
Releases and gives flight to broken winged birds.

Too Busy

"Too busy," this life.
My garden so overgrown
Begs me come visit

Ecology of Hope

Magnificent creation, courier of our truth,
I marvel at your incontrovertible message.
Writ within one small foot of your rich soil,
An earthen broadcast of corrective revelation.

Deep within this rich, layered, complex loam
Thousands of life forms thrive and mingle,
Reminding us who labor in topside gardens
Of this evidence-based, organic Good News:
All of life is interrelated and interdependent.

One multitude of different potent organisms
Pulse and proclaim, as prophets still ought:
"Incontestable diversity! Inestimable worth!"
The canard of sameness has been uprooted.

Deference

On the shore, gulls flock
I do not stir lest they leave:
Silent concordance

Tara

An ebony flash
Madly bolts across new snow:
Happy winter dog!

Clever Dog

Black lab on my bed
Are you or am I the guest?
Greedy canine knows

The Domicile Dialogues

I.

My house spoke
To me last night
At an annoyingly
Inconvenient hour.
"Ahem!" It coughed,
With loud pop
Emanating from
Some deep rib.
"What's that?"
I startled,
Heart pounding,
Not knowing
What might
Come next.
Then, House fell
Back to sleep
While I stared
Bleary-eyed at
The door knob.

II.

In winter,
House cannot
Bring hot tea.
Instead, I get,
"Here you go:
Heat's coming,"
Or so the
Creaking floors
Seem to suggest.
Still, I grab
My Aran throw.
Old House
Takes offense
At my chill,
Then bangs
the pipes
To hurry
A delivery
Of comfort.

III.

"VA-ROOSH!"
Bellows House
With such force
The walls shudder.
Black dog snaps
To attention at
Such roaring,
Looking to me
For answers.
"It's wicked
Out there, pal.
We'll be alright."
She believes,
But tucks behind
The old sofa
Just in case.
House flexes
Its muscles:
"We're good."

IV.

In summer,
A low rhythmic
Hum drifts into
My drowsy ear,
A soft, balmy
lyrical tune
From the south.
"Here, you'll
Like this,"
Whispers House
And begins
To softly croon
A dreamy
Melody
Of conjunct
And disjunct
Motion which
Lulls me into
Deep sleep.

Walking Oxford Conservation Park

I.
O infinite Mystery
Of beginnings, sustainings and endings,
When my last days approach
Kindly arrange for me to be here
Under the great Atlantic skyway
Within the parentheses
Of autumn and winter
When geese cronk above
Calling to me to follow

II.
What kind soul donated these eighty six acres
Of conserved land protecting our natural resources,
That you and I may stroll unconditionally into paradise?

Here, no pearly gates but salt meadow cordgrass,
Thickets of reeds, buttercups, milkweed and bergamot;
Paths revealing nocturnal prints of paws and hooves.

Here, no grand River Styx but the humble Tred Avon,
Daughter of the Choptank River, advancing and receding
With her lithesome form curling in from Town Creek.

Here, no scrutiny by Peter to get our tickets punched,
Just milder minions to welcome wanderers: Goldfinches,
Indigo buntings, meadow larks, and great blue herons.

III.
Runners, walkers, cyclers
Thread in and out
Of these fields,
Healthier for having done so.
For all such efforts,
What is exercised most
Is the soul.

The Waterman's Son

My friend steps
Where Algonquins once trod,
Sluicing barefoot into the Choptank
Sauntering to an oyster bar's velvety mound
Just two hundred feet from his porch.
His Bermuda hems kiss the tide,
Cueing bare feet to read the riverbed
Like braille, toeing and loosening
The first salt water bivalves
Soon to become tonight's meal.
With manicured hands, dinner is scooped
Without tongs, dredge or culling board.

A flash of guilt zips through him,
Much like a quick glint
Of minnows in the know.
They've felt tremors of diesel engines
Cutting through deeper waters at three a.m.
Steered by sleep-deprived men and women
Working the water for sweet mollusks,
For palates which fast in months having no "r's,"
Then salivate in ones that do.
No bills go unpaid or
College dreams get deferred
If his catch of the day is small.

Two masts, a mutton leg mainsail
Made the only office
His waterman father knew
Where dress code was a jacket of strength,
Bibs of patience, suspenders of luck.

His skipjack's hard chine hull plowed
Through all weather with ever lighter loads.
The law of diminishing returns,
His hungry stowaway,
Devoured drive and funds
Stripping skipper down to steely resolve
That his boy's life will not repeat his own.

A son's eye can embed in the brain
Paternal images that hide
Till death stirs them:
The toss of the old man's cap
Inside the door, bald head gray-blue with cold;
His sweaty, bronze dome bouncing sun's rays
From aboard his Queen of the Bay;
The hunch of shoulders when a day
Of gut-busting dredging yielded not enough;
Salt water puddling his rims
As he reads his son's name
On the college diploma.

Returning home
With a net's bounty of fresh oysters,
The son wades and meditates.
A rising tide of gratitude lifts away
Any qualms about a life easier than his father's.
He knows hard work, a gift of father to son,
Is the jib directing his fortune's winds.
Skipper in his own right,
He's leaned into all seas
As deftly as he'd been taught.
Looking out at the westerly setting sun,
Silhouettes of old watermen seem to wave.

Plein Air Mysteries

Some artists shock us with beauty
But we know not how.
Something sweeps through our eyes
Coasts into our spirit
Through the hands of these old souls
Whose brushes,
Loaded with ancient energy
Must tremble in that split second
Before touching canvas
As over and round their sable-haired wands
Drifts the same sacred breath of creation
Which has wended its way
To where each stands before easel.

One True Church

Neither wood nor stone
Build sacred space;
Hearts and minds
Make it so.

Talitha, Kum!

"Little girl, stand up!"

Imagine all the vibrant history
Silenced and suspended
Out of sight,
Out of mind,
Out of reach
For a millennium
Over every woman's head
Until finally,
Melted by the inextinguishable
Flame of discovery,
It now drips and pours and floods
Into bold passionate souls who,
Refusing to be spoken for,
Cry "Holy!"
Whenever, wherever they will.

Examination of Consciousness

Whose rules are these by which I've lived?
What random presupposition of circumstance
Has dictated such a tyranny as perfection,
Whose only begotten child is self-doubt?

What lost opportunities ennobled as "sacrifice"
Have been accrued because some iron mantle,
Laid upon young sloped, subordinate shoulders
By ten million brothers decreed "greater" than I,
Kept arms from reaching, heart from dreaming?

Those unconscious, obsequious days are no more.

Religious Imagination

Be careful with your invitation
To think outside the box,
To play apart from miters,
To dream beyond a cross.
Your guests may scandalize
Or threaten, perhaps even crack
Lichen-thick medieval walls
Where shafts of light
Bolt through your petrified stone,
Illuminating the path of equal regard
Long obscured by the detritus of refusal.

What Matters

These things matter most:
A self that can be selfless;
Deeds that free, not bind

Rats in Hats

The Barque has capsized
Thousands of children engulfed
Rats in hats scurry

How Many Good Fridays?

As if our guts had not been splayed enough
That bright, bleak Autumn of two thousand and one
When towers fell, markets crashed, dreams crumbled,
Then slammed upon us a scarlet tsunami of pedophilia.
Our trusting souls nearly drowned, awash in disbelief.
We clung to our battered boat, wild eyes searching
For some prophet to come toward us walking on water
Dripping in courage to save our sad broken barque.

Instead, Advent's rote message, "Wait in hope,"
Followed by Spring's Lenten joke, "Repent!"
Year after year, after every collusive, criminal year
My soul, in justice-parched delirium, envisioned this:
Liturgical dramas of basilica or cathedral proportions
Finally laying bare the espoused Grain of Wheat story:
The falling to ground, dying drop required for rebirth.
Ecclesial conspirators, how else venerate that cross?

No Advent, no Christmas, no Lent, no Easter
Has seen mitered men lay down their coveted lives
To repent the amassment of ruined, robbed children
Poor lambs to slaughter by wolves of moral blindness.
Lay down your crooked croziers which do not shepherd!
Lay down your pectoral crosses hung on fearful, faint hearts!
Lay down your bishops' rings on reluctant resignations!

What greater love could such hierarchy possibly preach?

Clash

Thoughtful, reflective, vocal;
Angry, strident, shrill;
Confessing anecdote histories;
Pitching prejudicial spin;
Releasing in spoken word
Sealing with unspeakable disdain
The power to heal each other
The refusal to be healed.

Nesters

Nesters, high and safe,
Will you stay and merely watch
Or decide and step up?

Reverend Tara

My dog is my priest.
Her daily gospel: "Let's go!"
Such, the voice of God

Niños Desesperados, Obispos

(Desperate Children, Bishops)

What is it about protecting children that you refuse to get?
Sexual abuse, physical abuse, verbal and emotional abuse,
Mental and psychological abuse, financial, economic abuse,
Cultural, identity abuse of children just are not your thing.

Where are you, cowardly prelates? Grubbing for tee time?
Wringing hands, hoping for VIP tickets to fat-cat fund raisers,
Fawning over political figures with cojones bigger than yours,
Souls shrunken as much as yours, morality as fickle as yours?

Caviling at the word cojones? "*How dare she say 'cojones'!*"
How dare a bishop utter "fetus," then leave the born to rot!
You can winter-march in cashmere coats for the right to life,
Yet do not march in indignation for formed bodies, caged.

"Suffer not the little children," torn from their mothers' arms,
Drinking from toilets, freezing on cement floors, unbathed,
Living in squalor, crying with hunger, terrified with uncertainty.
Are you blind to the inhumanity allowed in this shameful place?

Twenty seven hundred niños await the rustle of your cassocks.

Refugee

Amena, Benesh, Uduru, Pann, Faduma,
In your wombs, on your backs, on your hips, in your arms
You carry your children more miles than most think possible.
Syria, Afghanistan, South Sudan, Myanmar and Somalia
The lands which have bombed, beaten and defiled you
Have forced you into the bleakest recess of the heart: Grief.

Amena, Benesh, Uduru, Pann, Faduma,
Despots have imposed on you the language of goodbye,
An excruciating lexicon of loss in which you are too fluent.
Mothers, daughters, sisters, grandmothers, aunts, wives
No more honored as these, your identity is reviled refugee,
Powerless cypher, wandering with twenty-five million women.

Amena, Benesh, Uduru, Pann, Faduma
Your sisters who are free are rising and running to you
Do not despair before our arms encircle you, give you rest.
From you we will lift your children, feed, bathe, clothe them
Then turn to you with tenderness and caring long forgotten.
For, surely, we who champion human dignity outnumber despots,
Override bigots, usurp injustice and eclipse yawning indifference.

Here We Meet

Here we meet upon this bridge
Which reaches heaven to earth
A visible mingling of mercy and truth,
Of kindness and human worth.

You and I along this arc
Which spans the changing tides
Are stirred by grace to be lanterns lit
At one another's side.

For the Girls

Dear daughters of this millennium,
Come, settle for a while and listen.
Can you feel your breath slowing,
Sense your racing hearts calming?
Mothers, grandmothers, aunts of
The ages want to whisper to you,
Wrap around you the same cloak
Of courage once worn on their way.

You may think that you do not need
Such a pashmina of pluck quite yet;
May it ever be so, but allow these
Souls their nurturing bent to protect.
They are muses for us all and visit
Regularly in subtle winks and ways,
Nudging remembrance of the many
Shoulders upon which we now stand.

Should the old buzzsaw of inequality
Ever bear down on you, do not run!
Cry, "Seneca Falls!" and rally the girls
Until you break that terrible machine.
Elizabeth Katy Stanton, Lucretia Mott,
Susan B. Anthony resisted; so can you.
Sojourner Truth, Harriet Tubman knew
How to defy the biases of No with Yes!

When the fiery sting of outrage bites,
Take note: your future may be calling.
Wrongs ever will be in need of righting.
Here's to you who'll don judicial robes,
Lift the gavels of Sandra, Ruth, Sonia,
Elena and accede to their oak chambers.
Remember: Lady Justice is one of us,
Guarding fairness and equality in trials.

If it is said that you run or jump, throw
Or hit like a girl, chill, and thank the fool.
Flash him your pearly whites as tribute
To Olympians Joan Benoit, Simone Biles.
Recall the World Series' boys shut out by
Little league female pitcher, Mo'ne Davis.
"Hit like a girl?" Oh yes, please, just like
Chrissy, Serena, Venessa and Billy Jean.

Maybe designing is your unique imprint.
Louise Bethune, first woman architect,
Julia Morgan, designer of Hearst Castle,
Both dreamed, sketched and measured,
Drafting gutsy, innovative careers only
After crashing gates long closed to them.
Their seven hundred structures invite you:
Discover your talent, nurture it and thrive.

Perhaps circling the blue planet fires you.
You'll need a brilliant Katherine Johnson
Charting a trajectory for celestial dreams.
Youngest Astronaut, Sally Ride, launched
Beyond all the stars which carpet the sky,
Broadened Mae Jemison's own horizon
Into which she soared on orbiter, Endeavor.
Be that wise: the sky is no longer the limit.

There is no mother wishing less for you;
No grandmother will stifle proud cheers.
Aunts, another tier of steadfast support,
Join their voices to that maternal chorus:
You are beautiful and strong and good.
This is the lyric never to be forgotten,
The song to be carried in heart and soul.
You are beautiful and strong and good.

Pandemic

Forged from a mysterious genetic material
Far more formidable than any karat of gold,
A leaden diadem of death weighs humanity,
Buckles its knees under unforgiving gravity.

Corona of loss, this wild spiky protein shell,
One-thousandth the width of a mere eyelash,
Has proven mightier than powerful nations,
More efficient than bungling governments.

Clever as a cat-burglar sneaking undetected,
Co-vid breaks into cells wreaking its havoc
Making ten thousand copies of itself in hours,
Leaving victims and families limp, breathless.

The luxury of goodbye, a kiss before leaving
Are wishful thoughts that odds will not favor.
Strangers in scrubs, our unappointed proxies,
Tend now, our broken hearts folded in theirs.

An epidemic of arrogance has fed this virus.
Now, conversion squeezes through keyholes
Of closed minds, padlocked preconceptions
Only when the Reaper's made a personal call.

It's not so hard for humans to be noble, good;
But there's ease in choosing poorly, selfishly.
Still, our dark is dotted with millions of lights,
Beneficent beings who daily mend our souls.

Reluctant Walk

On the morning of the wake
I bought a pair of shoes:
Formal, serious slippers;
Designer somber,
Footwear for severance.

Those medium heels,
Had they sympathy with flesh,
Would have bled navy tears
Among my salty ones wept
At that lonely January plot.

Soft skinned companions,
Neither snow nor ice could stay us
From one more slide to graveside,
Delaying in the numbing cold
That uncertain gait of goodbye.

Winter shoes, they pinch me still.

Dear Weakened One

Oh dear weakened one
Your body so buffeted
Hearts wince at your plight

Fresh Pillow

Chemo exhaustion
Countered with human kindness:
Peace, a fresh pillow.

Mary and Elizabeth

The Visitation:
"I had to come when I heard."
"I knew that you would."

The Journey

This journey is yours.
I'll bring you poems and bread,
Carry your lantern.

Of Course

Easy going souls
As "of course" as stars and moon
Each, the other's sky

Few Words

Deeper, quieter
Our sacred space needs few words
We've pitched our tent here

The Storm

Again the dark storm.
My foundation, stronger now,
Will withstand what comes.

Bouquet

For our aching hearts
A bouquet of memories
Unfolding in time

What Eyes Cannot See

There are no starless nights
Passing clouds, averted eyes
Only make them seem so.
Sunless days are equal ruses,
The rain inviting such disbelief.

Memory holds the Northern lights,
The warmth of sun on skin,
Contradicting poor presumptions
That shadowed path or dreary bend
Are all that comprise this journey.

How necessary some sure reference,
Perhaps a compass in the hand;
Hope, a pivoting needle for guidance,
Aligned to so magnetic a Field
It quivers precisely the right path.

Fog and Night and T.S. Eliot

Fog and night:
How does one survive such a conspiracy?
My broken vessel, lurching in chaos,
Heaves and groans from swell to swell
As I hang on and wonder why.

Steady, steady:
Thick fog requires stillness,
Cupped ear, expectation.
Listen for signals; listen for safety;
Listen for the voice that sounds your rescue.

Dark ocean, dark sky:
I see, yet do not see in this miasmal mix.
Navigation succumbs to winds and currents,
To hand on tiller, to providence.
The chop of caring and not caring taunt me.

Fog and night:
Adrift on this uncharted sea of change
I hold on, remembering more than salty sea:
Fair weather follows storm; sun pierces dark.
The wide flung horizon gives bearing to port.

Freeing Lazarus

Jesus,
Having heard his friend was slipping,
Appeared by the wearied anxious
To have dallied a day or two.

"Too late," one of them whispered.
"Where were you?" the other,
Both spent from mourning
Their common loss.

Weeping over what he knew about tombs,
The Good Therapist drew out before them
The whole body of what had been buried
And kept so tightly under wraps.

Martha's warning was sound:
Too many days of not living
Does have a stench.

Deep behind that stone rolling miracle,
Life emerged again from God-knows-where.
Taking a cue from that redemptive wonder,
Each began the tender, slow process
Of untying and freeing.

Remembering Green

A soft rain, your voice,
Quenching this distant parched field
Which remembers green

Not Sun Nor Moon

Not a million stars
Not sun nor moon nor fire
Brighten as your eyes

Sunflower

For Janelle and Family

There is a road down which I need not travel, but I do.
A field of a thousand suns lures me on cloudless days.
This golden broadcast of helianthus, four acres long,
Imparts to the pausing seeker all that sunflowers know.

The planter of these yellow fields, their only perennial,
Pops up from under her straw hat when car doors thud.
Removing her gloves, she saunters over smiling widely,
Making visitors wonder if they'd met before but forgot.

Eventually, uncannily, she tells any disposed supplicants
A secret the sunflowers have charged her with delivering,
Not a proclamation to suggest a "crazy old lady" moniker,
But a gently woven story, tailored for their portable woes.

To a father, she describes the taproot, so strong it breaks
Through hardest soil, becoming an anchor in wild storms.
He shakes his head, mystified, that his fears of crumbling
Would be countered by the strength of one flower's stalk.

To a mother, Van Gogh is threaded into their casual chat.
"Did you know," the keen woman asks hidden bereft eyes,
"That the 'Painter of Sunflowers' told his friend, Gauguin,
He painted these as 'cry of anguish in the midst of thanks'?"

To the shy teen, she urges a walk by her side between rows,
Faces them east to twelve o'clock, while flowers face three.
"This is my field of discovery about growing, never settling:
A finite view is not all," say these, "brighter vistas beckon."

Dear Janelle, your synchronicity with sun crosses our sky.
While your petals and flowers turn toward Light every day,
We turn toward you, tracking your beauty within our hearts.
For love of you, we shall stand tall, heads up, and ever turn.

The Crowd on the Ledge

To have a dream then live it
One must have love.
Whether in the present pulsing moment
Or in the eternal one of memory,
Love is what reaches through all hesitation,
Fashioning wings which carry aloft:
One pinion for hope; the other, courage.

Speechless

A poem, you say?
Though my deep well is brimming
Words escape me so

Catherine's Way

(A Lesson from St. Catherine of Siena)

In this world, the cell of self knowledge
Remains the soul's recovery room.
Choice or circumstance bids us all enter
Though dark be the portal, above it the moon.

Pause here and rest in this place of discovery
That the eye of the intellect may focus anew
Upon all that is valued, sustaining, required
For life to be vibrantly, deliberately resumed.

Then be on the move like Catherine of Siena
In forward procession to the next and the next.
Curious to meet in each new encounter
That gift of grace when insight is blessed.

The Path

Ever Forward
Ever deeper
Leading to lighter
Ending with freer.
Blessed, the curious;
Brave, the eager.

Afterword

The poem on page forty-eight, "Fog and Night and T. S. Eliot," includes familiar references to Eliot's struggle with faith and adversity in his poem, "Ash Wednesday," published by Putnam in 1930.

About the Poet

Catherine R. Seeley's professional background includes health care administration; medical ethics; crisis, grief and transition. She also has been an educator/consultant for hospices, home health care agencies, long-term care facilities, hospitals, and health care systems around the country. Prior to her role as hospital vice president in Massachusetts, Catherine was director for bereavement services at a fully accredited two hundred bed palliative care specialty cancer hospital in New York for persons with advanced, acute cancer. A national and international lecturer, Catherine also has served on adjunct faculties at Iona College, St. Joseph College, Molloy College, and at Stony Brook University School of Medicine in New York. She is the author of articles in healthcare and ethics as well as a novel, *Mea Culpa*. Her article about the pandemic, "When Life Changes: Calming the Chaos of Crisis with Mindfulness," appears in the Fall 2020 volume of *Listening: Journal of Communication, Ethics, Religion and Culture*.

catherinerseeley.net

CPSIA information can be obtained
at www.ICGtesting.com
Printed in the USA
LVHW021448091120
671125LV00006B/979